W9-CHU-788

FIREFLIES

FIREFLIES

by Sylvia A. Johnson

Photographs by Satoshi Kuribayashi

A Lerner Natural Science Book

Lerner Publications Company ▪ Minneapolis

Sylvia A. Johnson, Series Editor

Translation of original text by Wesley M. Jacobsen

The publisher wishes to thank Jerry W. Heaps, Entomologist, for his assistance in the preparation of this book.

Photographs on page 7 by Isao Kishida. Drawings by Yoshitaka Moriue and Yooji Watanabe.

The glossary on page 46 gives definitions and pronunciations of words shown in **bold type** in the text.

LIBRARY OF CONGRESS CATALOGING-IN-PUBLICATION DATA

Johnson, Sylvia A.
  Fireflies.

  (A Lerner natural science book)
  Adaptation of: Hotaru/Satoshi Kuribayashi.
  Includes index.
  Summary: Describes the physical characteristics, habits, and natural environment of the soft-bodied member of the beetle family that uses its light to attract a mate.
    1. Fireflies—Juvenile literature. [1. Fireflies] I. Kuribayashi, Satoshi, 1939-   , ill. II. Kuribayashi, Satoshi, 1939-   , Hotaru. III. Title. IV. Series.
  QL596.L28J64   1986   595.76'44   86-26
  ISBN 0-8225-1485-0 (lib. bdg.)

This edition first published 1986 by Lerner Publications Company.
Text copyright © 1986 by Lerner Publications Company.
Photographs copyright © 1980 by Satoshi Kuribayashi.
Text adapted from FIREFLIES—THE SECRET OF THEIR LIGHT
copyright © 1980 by Satoshi Kuribayashi.
English language rights arranged by Japan Foreign-Rights
Centre for Akane Shobo Publishers, Tokyo, Japan.

International Standard Book Number: 0-8225-1485-0
Library of Congress Catalog Number: 86-26

1 2 3 4 5 6 7 8 9 10 96 95 94 93 92 91 90 89 88 87 86

Have you ever been fascinated by the greenish-yellow lights that flicker over lawns or meadows just after sunset on warm summer nights? Have you ever wondered what these tiny points of glowing light are and how they are created?

If you are like most people, you probably know that the mysterious lights are produced by small insects commonly called fireflies or lightning bugs. In this book, we will take a close look at the lives of these insects and examine the secret of their amazing natural light.

5

The 15 fireflies in this box were photographed by the glow of their own light.

WHAT ARE FIREFLIES?

The insects that produce the glowing light seen in the photograph above are popularly known as fireflies, but they are not really flies. They are beetles, members of the largest order within the insect world.

Fireflies belong to the beetle family Lampyridae and are distantly related to many familiar kinds of beetles such as ladybugs, water beetles, and scarab beetles. Like these insects, they have two pairs of wings but fly on only the second pair, using the first pair for balance in flight and as a protective covering when at rest. These unique protective wings, known as **elytra**, are typical of all beetles. They have inspired the scientific name for the order — Coleoptera, the sheath wings.

The order of beetles includes many varied and beautiful insects. The colorful ladybug (upper left) belongs to the beetle family Coccinellidae. Tiger beetles (upper right), members of the family Cicindelidae, are fierce, fast-flying predators. The family Carabidae is made up of long-legged beetles that spend most of their time hunting on the ground (lower left). Scarab beetles (lower right), like all their relatives, have transparent hind wings used for flying and hard front wings that serve as a protective covering.

MESSAGES OF LIGHT

Fireflies have sheath wings and many other things in common with their beetle relatives, but the one characteristic that is special to them is the ability to produce light. About two-thirds of the 2,000 species, or kinds, of fireflies within the family Lampyridae possess this ability as adults.

An adult firefly's light is produced by an organ called a **lantern**, located on the underside of the insect's abdomen. In many species of fireflies, the light does not glow steadily but flashes on and off in what seems to be a kind of code. Scientists have discovered that the insect's light is exactly that—a coded signal used to send messages to other fireflies.

The messages being sent by the flashing lights concern one of the most important subjects in the animal world—mating. Like all animals, fireflies must find mates of their own kind in order to carry out the vital job of reproduction. Many creatures, including other insects, locate and identify appropriate mates by means of smell. Fireflies use signals of light to find partners.

Fireflies usually begin their mating flights at dusk on spring or summer evenings.

Most fireflies set out to look for mates just after sunset on evenings in spring or early summer. The males fly along the edges of woods and fields or along streams. Female fireflies usually do not seek their mates on the wing. In fact, the females of some species, often referred to as **glowworms**, are wingless and unable to fly. Females usually perch on leaves or grass stems, looking for a familiar signal flashing in the night sky.

Each species of firefly seems to have its own special light signal that can be recognized by all members of the group. Scientists have been able to decipher about 130 of these coded signals. Some are very simple, consisting of a single flash of light repeated at regular intervals. Others are more complicated groups of flashes that vary in brightness and speed like a kind of visual Morse code.

Male fireflies flashing their lights as they fly along a stream bed. This photograph and others in the book are time exposures that show the insects' blinking lights as streaks and lines.

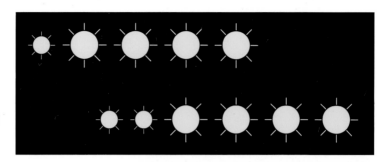

MALE

FEMALE

When a female responds to a male's signal, she waits for a few seconds before shining her own light. This pause seems to be important in distinguishing the signals of different fireflies species.

MALE

FEMALE

When a female firefly sees the signal of a male of her species, she responds by flashing her own light. The codes of most females are series of short pulses that do not usually vary in brightness. What seems to be the main difference among the female signals is the timing.

A female will wait for a specific amount of time before responding to a male signal. This brief pause before answering the male's invitation seems to be the message that identifies the female as an appropriate mate, that is, as a member of the same species. If the answer comes too soon or too late, then the male knows that it comes from a female who is not a potential partner.

The light signals of some female fireflies can be invitations to disaster.

Sometimes a female's message of light is not a response to the male's mating proposal but an invitation to disaster. The females of at least one group of fireflies (members of the North American genus *Photuris*) use a false message to lure male fireflies to a banquet at which they are the main course.

Most adult fireflies are not **carnivorous**, but many *Photuris* females do feed on flesh, especially on other fireflies. While these females don't usually eat members of their own species, they are eager to get their jaws on other kinds of fireflies. To obtain a meal, they imitate the female response message of another firefly species, luring the unsuspecting males to them.

Many of these predatory females can imitate the message of only one other species, but several are capable of responding to at least five different kinds of male fireflies. These versatile mimics wait on the ground until they see a male flashing its signal, and then they answer with the appropriate female response. In many cases, they are successful in fooling the male and in getting a meal.

Although some exchanges of firefly messages end in disaster, many more lead to a peaceful meeting between the insects. Flying in a zigzag pattern toward the female's perch, the male firefly repeats his invitation over and over. The female continues to respond until the male finally reaches her side. The insects mate quickly, and then the male takes off again to seek a new partner. The female too leaves her perch, not to look for another mate but to get ready for her next task in the process of reproduction.

A male firefly cautiously approaches a female (inset picture) and then mates with her. As in many groups of insects, male fireflies are usually smaller than their mates.

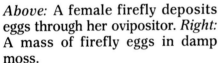
Above: A female firefly deposits eggs through her ovipositor. *Right:* A mass of firefly eggs in damp moss.

FROM EGG TO LARVA

About five to six days after mating, the female fireflies are ready to lay the eggs that have been developing inside their bodies. Emiting pulses of light, they fly to damp areas, often near water, to deposit their eggs. Other females attracted by the lights may gather at the same spots.

Egg laying usually takes place during the dark hours of the night and may continue for several nights. Each female lays about 500 eggs, but some may produce as many as 1,000. The eggs leave the insect's body through a tube called an **ovipositor**, which extends from the tip of the abdomen. As each egg passes out of the female's body, it is fertilized by the male sperm that has been stored since the time of mating.

These female fireflies are laying their eggs in moss growing on rocks near a river. The moss keeps the eggs moist and protects them from the sun. While they lay their eggs, the fireflies continue to produce pulses of glowing light.

NOTE: The insects shown in this photograph and throughout the book belong to the species *Luciola vitticollis*, which is native to Asia. The life cycle described in the following pages, while typical of many kinds of fireflies, is based on the particular habits of this species.

Adult fireflies die soon after mating, victims of predators like spiders (above) or simply of old age.

The female fireflies do not live long after they have finished laying their eggs. Like most insects, their adult lives are very short, usually no more than four weeks. Their partners, the male fireflies, are all dead by this time, and the females too will die quietly in the bushes after their important job is done.

In the eggs they leave behind, however, a new generation of fireflies is developing. And inside the eggs, the fireflies-to-be have begun to produce the mysterious light for which their family is famous.

Above left: Firefly eggs shortly after being laid. They are only half a millimeter in diameter—not much bigger than the point of a pencil. *Above right:* Eggs about 20 days after laying. The fireflies developing inside can be seen through the eggs' transparent covering. *Below:* Firefly eggs often glow with a dim, steady light. Scientists do not know what purpose the firefly's light serves at this stage of its life.

A firefly larva hatching from its egg. First the larva bites through the egg covering and sticks its head out (left). Then it pushes its upper body through the opening (center) and uses its legs to pull the rest of its long body out of the egg (right).

LARVAL DEVELOPMENT

About one month after the eggs were laid, the young fireflies inside are ready to emerge. On a dark mid-summer night, they bite through the tough, flexible eggshells and make their way out into the world.

The newly hatched fireflies are strange-looking little creatures with long, worm-like bodies that look nothing like the winged forms of adult fireflies. Like many insects, fireflies go through several very different stages of development on their way to becoming adults. This process of growth is called **metamorphosis**, a word that means "transformation."

When the fireflies emerge from their eggs, they have entered the **larval** stage of their transformation. In their worm-like forms, the insects are known as **larvae** (singular, larva). The fireflies will spend more time in this stage of metamorphosis than in any other period of their lives.

With their segmented, worm-like bodies, firefly larva look nothing like the winged adults of their species.

Firefly larvae float on the surface of a river or stream (opposite) and then sink to the bottom, where they hide under rocks (left) or walk along looking for food (right). While underwater, the larvae breathe through tube-like gills on their abdomens (inset picture opposite).

Many firefly larvae live on land, scurrying through the litter of leaves and hiding in burrows in the soil. Some, however, spend their larval period underwater. The species of firefly shown in these photographs belongs in this group.

As soon as the larvae emerge from their eggs, they move toward the nearby river or stream. Those that hatched on the river bank tumble right into the water.

After reaching their watery homes, the larvae first float on the surface and then begin twisting and bending until they gradually sink to the bottom. Here they move around by walking with the three pairs of legs attached to the **thorax**, the middle section of their segmented bodies. They breathe through tube-like gills that extend from the segments of their long **abdomens**.

23

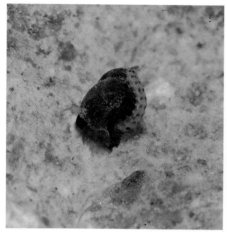

A larva attacks a snail by grabbing its shell (above), but the animal breaks free and escapes (right).

Whether they live in water or on land, firefly larvae have one primary activity—looking for food. The larval stage is the main period of growth in the insects' lives, and they need large amounts of food to fuel their development.

Many firefly larvae find the nourishment they need in a diet of snails. Both land snails and freshwater snails supply food for hungry larvae. The insects creep up on the snails and seize the animals' soft bodies with their sharp **mandibles**, or jaws. Even if a snail withdraws into its shell, a larva is usually able to hang on.

In order to consume its meal, the larva injects the snail with digestive juices that dissolve its body. Then the larva simply sucks the softened material out of the snail's shell.

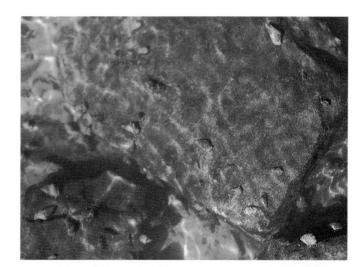

Right: Freshwater snails are an important part of a firefly larva's diet. *Below:* These two larvae have captured a snail and are feeding on its soft body with their heads inside the shell.

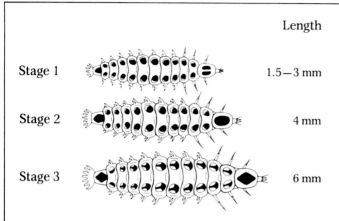

	Length
Stage 1	1.5 — 3 mm
Stage 2	4 mm
Stage 3	6 mm

Opposite: When a larva molts, it bends and twists its body until its old skin splits (1, 2, 3). Then it wiggles out of the old skin, revealing the new, lighter skin underneath (4, 5). About 12 hours later, a pattern of dark markings begins to appear on its body (6).

These drawings show the first three stages of a larva's development.

Like all insects in the larval stage, a firefly larva has a big appetite, and the large quantities of food it consumes cause it to grow rapidly. This growth is very different from the gradual development of other kinds of animals.

A larva's growth takes place in separate stages, each marked by **molting**, or shedding of the insect's skin. Unlike the skin of other animals, a larva's skin does not expand. In order for its body to grow larger, the old skin must be shed to make way for the new, larger skin that develops underneath.

All insects go through several molts during their larval period. The firefly species shown here molts six times, the first molt coming about a month after hatching. Each time the larva sheds its skin, its body becomes larger and changes slightly in appearance. The photographs on the opposite page show a firefly larva going through its third molt.

26

Left: A firefly larva's large hook-shaped jaws allow it to get a good grip on its prey. *Right:* This larva has white poison glands that it uses to defend itself against predators.

Even after its third molt, the firefly larva is a tiny creature, less than 10 millimeters (about 0.7 inches) in length. Its small size makes it very vulnerable to predators.

Whether firefly larvae live on land or in the water, they are threatened by animals that hunt and eat them in the same way that the larvae prey on snails. Birds feed on firefly larvae as well as on caterpillars, which are the larval forms of butterflies and moths. In or near water, fish, frogs, and toads make meals of any larvae that come their way.

A larva's best defense against being eaten is to stay out of sight. During the day, larvae hide under rocks or leaves, coming out only during the dark hours of night to hunt. Some firefly larvae have special means of self-defense in the form of glands that secrete a poisonous fluid. This poison makes the insects an unappealing meal to predators.

A larva seizes a snail (above) and hides under a rock while eating it (below).

A firefly can even keep out of sight when feeding on a snail. With its head inside the snail's shell, the larva hides the rest of its body under rocks. Any predator searching for a meal would see only the snail shell, not realizing that the larva was feasting inside it.

When it has finished its development, a larva leaves the water (left) and moves out on the moist soil of the river bank (right).

FROM LARVA TO PUPA

The firefly larvae that hatched from their eggs and entered the stream in mid-summer spend the autumn and winter underwater. (Larvae that stay on land have a different kind of schedule.) By the time that spring arrives, the insects have completed their larval development and are ready to move on to the next stage of metamorphosis.

The next period of their growth will take place on land. On a rainy spring night, the larvae leave the water and move out onto the moist soil of the river bank. As they crawl along, they produce an unblinking light, as they did from time to time during their underwater existence. (Firefly larvae are sometimes called glow-worms because of their ability to produce light.)

The lights of firefly larvae that are moving along the edge of the river. Most larvae are able to produce light, but they do not seem to use it as a signal in in the way that adult fireflies do.

A larva burrows into the damp soil in preparation for the next stage in its development.

Once out of the water, a larva looks for a small hole or hollow in the soft soil. When it finds an appropriate spot, it burrows in head first to a depth of 3 to 7 centimeters (about 2 to 4.5 inches) and begins making a chamber by pushing the soil aside. The larva's body secretes a liquid that soaks into the walls of the chamber. When the liquid hardens, it forms a waterproof coating for the underground room.

After it has finished its work, the larva curls up and rests quietly. Even in the darkness of the earth, its lantern glows softly.

The cross-section photographs on this page show a larva's underground chamber. In the picture above, the larva hollows out the chamber and secretes a fluid that soaks into its walls.

The photograph on the upper right gives an exterior view of the hardened wall of the chamber. On the lower right, you can see the larva resting and waiting for the great change that is to take place.

After its final molt, the larva is transformed into a pupa, the third stage in its metamorphosis.

Buried in its underground chamber, the larva remains motionless for several weeks. During this time, the spring sun warms the world outside, and other insects become active along the river banks.

Finally, about 40 days after it entered its protective chamber, the larva begins to stir. It straightens out from its curled-up position and twists its body until a split opens in its skin. The larva has begun its sixth and final molt.

The creature that emerges from the molted larval skin is a **pupa,** the third stage in the firefly's metamorphosis. This period is in many ways the most remarkable in the insect's development. During the pupal stage, the parts of the larva's body will be broken down and reformed into the body of an adult insect.

34

After the larval skin is shed, the pupa rests while a hard, transparent shell forms over its body. Even at this stage, the wings and other body parts of an adult firefly have begun their development and can be seen through the pupal covering.

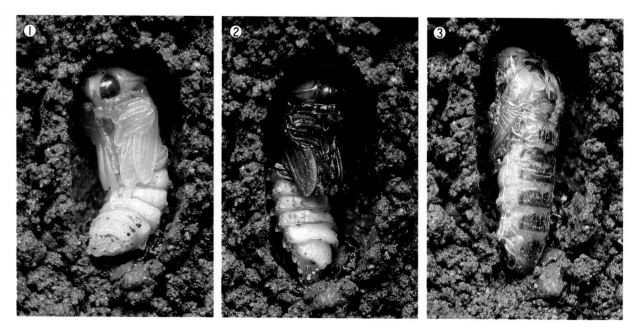

The photographs on these two pages show some of the stages in the development of a firefly pupa.

EMERGENCE OF THE ADULT FIREFLY

The firefly pupa stays in its underground chamber for about 10 days, remaining motionless while its metamorphosis continues. At the end of this period, the pupa begins moving. It stretches and bends its body until the pupal shell splits at the back. The insect works its way out of the shell, using its legs to push the transparent covering down to the bottom of the chamber.

The creature that emerges from the pupal covering is a fully developed adult firefly, complete with two pairs of wings and all the other adult body parts. Metamorphosis has been completed, and the firefly is ready to begin its short life as an adult.

1) On the 7th day after the development began, the pupa's large eyes have become black, and its developing wings are wrapped around its body. 2) By the 9th day, the wings and upper body have darkened. 3) On the 10th day, the pupal shell splits, and the insect begins to emerge. 4) Ten minutes later, half the firefly's body is out of the shell, and its wings have begun to straighten out. 5) Thirty minutes after the shell split, the adult firefly has completely emerged. It moves its first pair of wings to dry out the second pair folded up beneath them. 6) About 15 hours after emerging from the pupal shell, the firefly has completed its development. Its upper wings have turned the normal adult color, and the insect is ready to emerge from the earth.

An adult firefly leaves its underground chamber (left) and then rests on a plant, spreading its two pairs of wings (right).

After becoming an adult, the firefly stays in its underground chamber for several days, resting and regaining its strength after the struggle to escape from the pupal covering. Then it is time to leave the chamber for the outside world. The firefly chews through the wall of the chamber with its mandibles and then pushes its way to the surface with its legs. If the ground is hard, the insect may not be able to escape and will die in its dark cell.

If the firefly does succeed in breaking out, it rests for a while on a nearby plant before flying toward the stream, where other fireflies are also gathering. In a very short time, it will begin its search for a mate, using the flashing signals peculiar to its own species.

An adult firefly takes in moisture from dewdrops on a blade of grass. Most fireflies eat no food during their adult lives. During this short period, they survive on the nourishment stored during the long larval stage of their development.

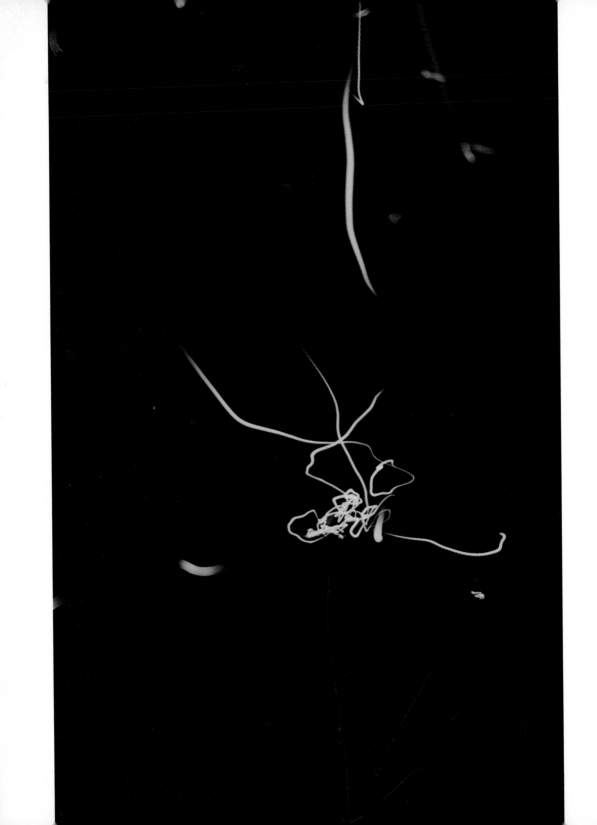

Fireflies are only one of the creatures able to produce their own light.

THE SECRET OF THE FIREFLY'S FIRE

The firefly's signals are remarkable not only because of the role they play in the insect's life but also because of the way they are produced. Scientists who study fireflies have learned that the beetles' "fire" is a product of **bioluminescence**, the ability of living things to create light by means of a chemical reaction.

A surprising number of creatures possess this remarkable ability. Most of the light-makers live in the ocean, at depths below 90 meters (300 feet). Many fish and other deep-sea animals can light their own way through the darkness, attracting mates or prey and frightening away predators. In addition to fireflies, there are several kinds of insects that bioluminesce. Most of them are beetles, including the spectacular railroad worm, a wingless female beetle that has a row of lights along each side of her body and a glowing red "headlamp."

41

The exact location of a firefly's lantern depends on the insect's species and sex. In the species shown here *(Luciola vitticollis)*, the male's lantern is in the last two segments of the abdomen (left), while the female's is in the second last segment (right).

Scientific studies have shown that most of these bioluminescent creatures produce light in basically the same way. It is a result of a chemical reaction involving two different substances, known as **luciferin** and **luciferase**. (Both terms are derived from the Latin word *lucifer*, which means "light-bearing.") Luciferin is a chemical compound that reacts with oxygen to produce the light; luciferase is an enzyme that makes the reaction possible.

Unlike other bioluminescent lights, the firefly's fire requires one additional ingredient, **adenosine triphosphate** (ATP), a compound found in the cells of all living things. This substance must first react with the luciferin before the other chemical reactions can take place.

The chemical process occurs in a firefly's lantern, located on the underside of the abdomen. The lantern is a complicated organ technically known as a **photophore** (light-carrier). It is made up of several layers of cells. One layer consists of **photocyte** cells, where the essential chemicals are produced and the reaction takes place. Another layer consists of **reflector** cells that direct and intensify the light. Surrounding these groups of cells are air passages that bring in the oxygen required by the light-making process.

42

A firefly pupa's light glows brightly but does not flash.

The flashing of the firefly's light seems to be controlled by the insect's nervous system. Nerve impulses are transformed into chemical messages that communicate with the photocytes, starting the chemical reaction or turning it off.

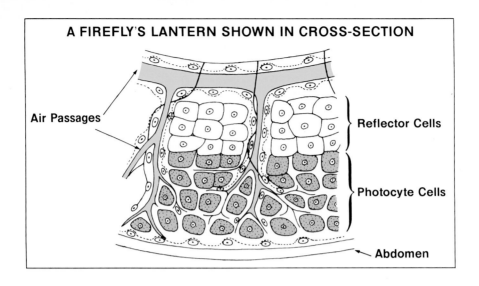

A FIREFLY'S LANTERN SHOWN IN CROSS-SECTION

Air Passages

Reflector Cells

Photocyte Cells

Abdomen

Scientists have learned a great deal about the firefly's light-producing ability, but they still have many unanswered questions. Some of the puzzles are related to the basic principle of bioluminescence and its existence in the animal world. Unlike light created by humans, bioluminescent light is "cool." Almost no heat is produced as part of the light-making process. If humans could master the secret of creating cool light, it would be a significant scientific discovery.

Research on fireflies has already produced some important findings. Scientists have discovered that the insects' light-producing chemicals may be useful in detecting disease in human cells. When luciferin and luciferase are combined with blood samples containing bacteria, the chemicals produce a bright light in reaction to the high amounts of ATP caused by the presence of the bacterial cells. Because cancerous cells seem to contain less ATP than normal, these same chemicals produce a weak light when combined with samples containing such abnormal cells.

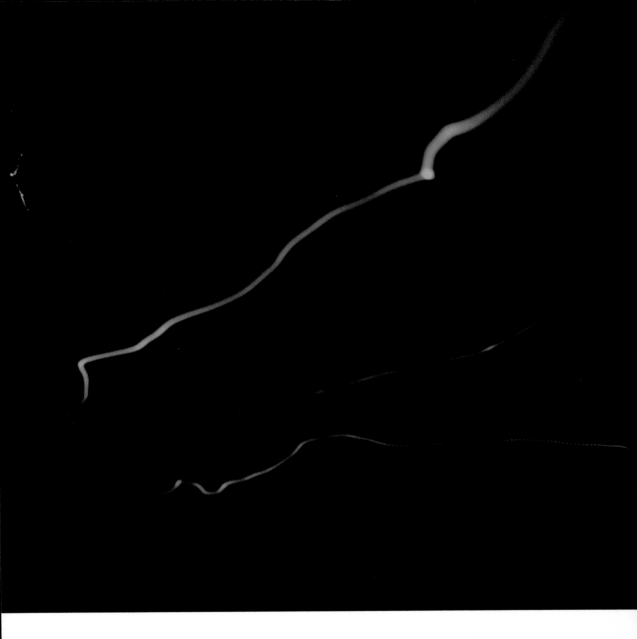

If this kind of research eventually leads to practical results, then the firefly's light may come to play as important a role in the human world as it does in the natural cycle of the insect's life.

GLOSSARY

abdomen—the third part of an insect's body, containing the digestive and reproductive organs

adenosine triphosphate (eh-DEN-uh-seen tri-FAHS-fate)—a chemical compound, found in the cells of all living things, that plays a part in the production of a firefly's light

bioluminescence (bi-oh-loo-meh-NES-ehntz)—the ability of living things to produce light by means of a chemical reaction

carnivorous—flesh-eating

elytra (eh-LIE-truh)—the hard front wings of beetles, which serve as covers for the hind wings. The singular form of the word is **elytron**.

glowworms—a name often used to refer to firefly larvae and the wingless females of some firefly species

lantern—the organ on a firefly's abdomen where light is produced

larvae (LAR-vee)—insects in the second stage of complete metamorphosis. The singular form of the word is **larva (LAR-vuh)**.

luciferase (loo-SIF-eh-ras)—an enzyme that sets off the chemical reaction in a firefly's lantern

luciferin (loo-SIF-eh-ruhn)—a chemical compound that reacts with oxygen to produce the firefly's light

mandibles (MAN-dih-bl's)—an insect's jaws

metamorphosis (met-uh-MOR-fuh-sis)—the process of growth and change that produces most adult insects. Beetles, bees, ants, and many other kinds of insects go through a four-stage development known as **complete metamorphosis**: the four stages are egg, larva, pupa, and adult. Another process of development called **incomplete metamorphosis** has only three stages: egg, nymph, and adult.

molting—the process of shedding an old skin to make way for a new, larger skin that has developed underneath

ovipositor (oh-vee-POS-ih-tur)—a tube at the end of a female insect's abdomen through which eggs leave the body

photocyte (FOT-uh-site)—one of the cells in a firefly's lantern where the light-producing chemical reaction takes place

photophore (FOT-uh-fore)—a light-producing organ such as a firefly's lantern

pupa (PEW-puh)—an insect in the third stage of complete metamorphosis. The plural form of the word is **pupae (PEW-pee)**.

reflector—a cell in a firefly's lantern that directs and focuses light produced by the photocytes

thorax (THOR-aks)—the middle part of an insect's body, to which the legs are attached

INDEX

abdomen, 8, 22, 42
adenosine triphosphate
   (ATP), 42, 44
adult firefly, emergence of,
   36-37, 38

beetles, 6-7, 8
bioluminescence, 41-44

carnivorous fireflies, 14
Coleoptera, 6

eggs: laying of, 16;
   development of, 19, 20;
   hatching of, 20

female fireflies, signals of,
   13, 14

gills, 22
glowworms, 10, 30

ladybugs, 6, 7
Lampyridae, 6, 8
lantern, 8, 42
larvae, 20, 22; development
   of, 26, 28, 30, 32, 34;
   food of, 24, 29; predators
   of, 28
lifespan of adult fireflies, 18
light of fireflies: during
   larval stage, 30, 32;
   patterns of, 10, 13;
   production of, 8, 41-44;
   purpose of, 8-9; research
   on, 41, 42, 44-45
luciferase, 42, 44
luciferin, 42, 44

Luciola vitticollis (firefly
   species), 17, 42

male fireflies, signals of, 10,
   13, 14
mandibles, 24
mating, 9, 10, 13, 15
medical research on fire-
   flies, 44-45
metamorphosis, 20; larval
   stage of, 20, 26, 30, 34;
   pupal stage of, 34, 36
molting, 26, 28, 34

ovipositor, 16

photocyte, 42, 43
photophore, 42
Photuris (firefly genus), 14
poison glands, 28
predators of fireflies, 28
predatory fireflies, 14
pupae: development of, 35,
   36, 38; emergence of, 34

railroad worm, 41
reflector cells, 42
reproduction, 9, 15, 16

scarab beetles, 6, 7
sheath wings, 6, 8
snails, 24, 29

thorax, 22
tiger beetles, 7

water beetles, 6